SHONEN JUMP MANGA EDITION

BLACK CAT

ブラック・キャット

VOLUME 8

CERBERUS STRIKES

STORY & ART BY KENTARO YABUKI

characters
BLACK CAT
TRAIN HEARTNET
SVEN VOLLFIED
SAYA MINATSUKI
RINSLET WALKER
ZAGINE
EVE
CHRONO NUMBERS
No. II BELZE
No. I SEPHIRIA
No. V NIZER
No. XI BELUGA
No. VII JENOS

APOSTLES of the STARS

A fearless "eraser" responsible for the deaths of countless powerful men, Train "Black Cat" Heartnet carries an ornate pistol called "Hades." The gun is engraved with the Roman numeral XIII, Train's agent number as an assassin for the crime syndicate Chronos, a mysterious organization that quietly controls one-third of the world's economy. Two years after his departure from Chronos, Train lives a carefree wanderer's life, working with his partner Sven as a bounty hunter ("sweeper") and pursuing Creed Diskenth, the man who murdered Train's beloved friend Saya. The two sweepers are allied with sexy thief-for-hire Rinslet Walker and Eve, a young girl (and experimental living weapon) whom they rescued from a nanotech lab.

Creed has formed a gang of killers, the "Apostles of the Stars," to revolt against Chronos and the world order. They staged an attack on a summit of world leaders, resulting in multiple assassinations. Chronos scrambled to respond, sending their top agent, Sephiria Arks, to Train for assistance, but she received no response. Soon thereafter, an Apostle named Durham got impatient and challenged Train directly. That move raised Creed's ire and he executed Durham for his impertinence, causing some unrest among the other members of the group. Meanwhile, Chrono Number VII hired Rinslet to locate the Apostles' safe house. Each organization has made its move, and the specter of war looms over their world.

BLACK CAT™

VOLUME 8 CERBERUS STRIKES

CONTENTS

chk
Thirteen Years Ago
Train Heartnet, Age 10
THE ART OF WAR
I never wavered ...
I *always* meant to kill him.
Chapter 68: Days of Youth

Chapter 68:
Days of Youth

WHAM
AHHHHH!
BLAM
AGH!
TUMBLE

K-TCHK
K-TCHK
SHATTER
UGH...
OW!

READ THIS WAY

YOU'VE GOT NO SHORTAGE OF ***BLOOD-LUST,*** I'LL GIVE YOU THAT MUCH!
TMP
TMP
HEH HEH HEH ...
HIS NAME WAS ZAGINE.
AND HE MURDERED MY PARENTS.
IN THE FOUR MONTHS SINCE THEIR DEATH ...
HE'D BEEN TEACHING ME THE ART OF THE ASSASSIN, STARTING WITH MARKS-MANSHIP.
TO THIS DAY, I DON'T KNOW WHAT HE HAD PLANNED.

READ THIS WAY
117...
118...
119...
WHAT'S THE MATTER?
STOP AND I'LL BLOW YOUR ARM OFF.
125...
126...!
CLACK...
DRINK UP.

IT'S MILK.
CREAK
...
I DON'T WANT IT.
JUST DRINK IT.
C'MON, NOW. IT'S TASTY *AND* NUTRITIOUS. IF YOU WANT TO BUILD UP YOUR STRENGTH, YOU'LL DRINK IT.
STRENGTH ...

READ THIS WAY
I HIT IT!
THAT IS NOTHING TO CHEER ABOUT, YOU FOOL KID.
BANG BANG BANG
...
ZAGINE WAS POWER-FUL.
AND HE NEVER MISSED HIS MARK.

LISTEN CARE-FULLY...
IN THIS WORLD, *POWER* IS EVERY-THING.
THE STRONGEST AMONG US CALL ALL THE SHOTS AND THE WEAK CANNOT COMPLAIN.
NEVER ALLOW YOUR-SELF TO BECOME DEPEN-DENT ON *ANYONE*.
THE *ONLY* PERSON YOU CAN ULTIMATELY RELY UPON IS *YOUR-SELF*.
THAT IS MY PHILOSOPHY.

TO ME...
ZAGINE SEEMED LIKE THE STRONGEST MAN IN THE WORLD.
I TRAINED *EVERY* DAY...
SLOWLY BUILDING UP MY STRENGTH...
...INTENT ON MATCHING ZAGINE'S POWER ONE DAY.
WITHOUT MY REALIZING IT...
...KILLING ZAGINE TO AVENGE MY PARENTS HAD BECOME MY *LIFE'S GOAL*.

...
ZAGINE...
ARE YOU...
ARE YOU BLEED-ING?

READ THIS WAY
...
I-IT APPEARS ...
I'VE JOINED THE RANKS OF *THE WEAK.*
NO--!
YOU CAN'T!
HOLD ON!!
SPLASH
IF YOU DIE NOW, I'LL NEVER BE SATISFIED!
HRMPH ...
SO YOU SET YOUR SIGHTS ON ME, DID YOU?
GRIN

IF YOU HOPE ONE DAY...
...TO SURPASS YOUR TEACHER ...
BEGIN BY LIVING ON YOUR OWN.
BANG
BANG
BANG
GROW STRONG.

BECOME STRONGER THAN ANYONE OR ANYTHING THAT YOU MIGHT ENCOUNTER. LIVE AS I HAVE TAUGHT YOU. YOU WILL SURVIVE...
...TRAIN HEARTNET!
THIRTEEN YEARS LATER--

...
CHK
TRAIN...
HEY, TRAIN!
WHAT?
YOU KNOW...
...YOU COULD GIVE US A HAND HERE.

READ THIS WAY
NAH, I DON'T THINK SO.
I'M A SWEEPER, NOT A MECHANIC! ♪
WHAT?! IF YOU THINK--!
IT'S OKAY, SVEN.
HUH?
IF HE DOESN'T WORK, HE DOESN'T EAT.
WE'LL JUST PUT TRAIN'S SHARE OF TODAY'S FOOD BUDGET TOWARD OUR LOAN PAYMENT.
WH-WHAT?!
ALL RIGHT, FINE!
I'LL HELP. SATISFIED?!

YOWZA!
ANYONE EVER TOLD YOU HAVE BEAUTIFUL EYES? ♡
LET'S YOU AND I GRAB SOME DINNER. WHAT DO YOU SAY?
I SAY, "FORGET IT!"
HUFF HUFF
...
MY, OH MY...
THEY DO HAVE SOME UPPITY WOMEN IN THIS TOWN.

READ THIS WAY

BLACK CAT

profile

ZAGINE AXELOAKE

DATA	
BIRTHDATE:	UNKNOWN
AGE:	43
BLOOD TYPE:	B
HEIGHT:	188 CM
WEIGHT:	89 KG
HOBBIES:	COLLECTING GUNS
COMMENTS:	ASSASSIN. ORPHANED AS A CHILD WHEN HIS PARENTS DIED IN AN ACCIDENT, ZAGINE MADE A GOOD LIFE FOR HIMSELF IN THE WORLD OF CRIME. THOUGH IT WAS HIS POLICY TO REFUSE CONTRACTS ON "TARGETS WITH YOUNG CHILDREN," THE CLIENT WHO HIRED HIM TO KILL TRAIN'S PARENTS PURPOSELY OMITTED THE FACT OF TRAIN'S EXISTENCE.

LEOL CITY STATION
CHAPTER 69: RINSLET'S ORDEAL
GIRLS, GIRLS, GIRLS!
WHAT'S YOUR HURRY ?!
WHY TAKE AN ORDINARY TRAIN...
...WHEN YOU CAN RIDE THE JENOS EXPRESS TO DESTINY?*
(*EVEN WE DON'T KNOW WHAT THAT MEANS. -- ED.)

HEH HEH I MEAN ...
THE THREE OF US COULD ...
CLENCH
HUH?
POW
DON'T YOU EVER GIVE UP?!
AHHH!!
WE'RE LEAVING!
DRAG
DRAG
...
UH...
WHAT WAS THAT?

Chapter 69:
Rinslet's Ordeal

TATAN
TATAN
COULD YOU PULL YOURSELF TOGETHER, PLEASE?
ALL YOU EVER DO IS HIT ON WOMEN!
MEANWHILE, *I'M* BUSTING MY BUTT TRYING TO FIND CREED-- WHO'S SUPPOSED TO BE *YOUR* TARGET!
HEE HEE.
YOU SURE ARE *UPSET.*

READ THIS WAY
ME-THINKS...
YOU'RE JEALOUS!
SPARK
GRGR
OKAY, OKAY! I GET THE MESSAGE. SHEESH.
TATAN
...
TATAN
ANYWAY. DON'T YOU THINK YOU OWE ME AN EXPLANATION?

I KNOW YOU WERE ORDERED TO DELIVER ME TO CASTORAL CITY.
BUT I DON'T KNOW *WHY.*
ER?
SEPHI WANTS TO MEET YOU.
SEPHI?
SEPHIRIA ARKS.
AGENT NUMBER *ONE.*

THE WOMAN THE CHRONOS ELDERS CHOSE TO LEAD THEIR ELITE TEAM OF ASSASSINS!
!
SCREECH
VROOM

ZAH
THAT'S ...
...

HER ?!
WATCH YOUR-SELF, RINS.
YOU DON'T WANT TO GET ON SEPHI'S BAD SIDE.
IT'S BEEN A WHILE.
YOU LOOK WELL, JENOS.
POW!
YOU KNOW IT!!
HEALTHY, HEARTY AND *RARING* TO GO!!

SO I SEE.
AND YOU MUST BE RINSLET WALKER.
HOW DO YOU DO? I AM AGENT ONE OF THE NUMBERS.
YOU MAY CALL ME...
OH, I GET IT!!
THIS IS ALL A BIG JOKE, RIGHT?!
C'MON! THERE'S NO WAY A LITTLE THING LIKE THAT COULD COMMAND THE NUMBERS!
JENOS, YOU KIDDER! YOU'RE PUTTING ME ON!!
HUH?

UH OH.
I SEE...
YOU'RE STILL QUITE YOUNG AREN'T YOU, RINSLET?
HUH?
IT'S ALL RIGHT. IT'S A COMMON FOLLY OF YOUTH TO JUDGE POWER BY PHYSICAL APPEARANCE.
GRIN☆
I'M NOT OFFENDED.
FOLLY?!
WAS THAT SUPPOSED TO BE SARCASTIC?
HOW DARE SHE?!

SIGN: TEAHOUSE HAKUSHU

READ THIS WAY
WELCOME.
WE HAVE BEEN EXPECTING YOU.
I AM QUITE FOND OF THIS PLACE. I FIND IT VERY *RELAXING*, DON'T YOU?
...

CLACK
NOW THEN ...
JENOS SUBMITTED THE DATA YOU COMPILED OVER THE LAST FEW WEEKS...
FOR MY REVIEW AND EVALUATION.
SLIIIDE
APOSTLES OF THE STARS--
KYOKO KIRISAKI...
AND CHARDEN FLAMBERG.

READ THIS WAY
CHRONOS PROVIDED YOU WITH A SINGLE PHOTO...
AND YOU WERE ABLE TO COMPILE EXTENSIVE DOSSIERS ON BOTH SUBJECTS.
AND VERY QUICKLY, AT THAT.
IMPRES-SIVE.
...
WHAT, THAT? THAT WAS NOTHING. I HAVE BEEN IN THE BUSINESS FOR EIGHT YEARS, AFTER ALL.
SMUG
WHY, I CAN'T TELL YOU HOW MANY TIMES I'VE HAD TO TRACK DOWN A TREASURE THAT COULD BE HIDDEN ANYWHERE IN THE WORLD AND ALL I'VE HAD TO GO ON WAS A PHOTO!

BE THAT AS IT MAY...
I NEEDED TO MAKE *SURE* WE COULD RELY ON YOU. I'M CERTAIN OF THAT NOW.
?!
WHOA! BACK UP.
SO THIS ...
...WAS SOME KIND OF *TEST*?

SLAM
HOW DARE YOU?!
I DON'T CARE WHAT NUMBER YOU ARE...
...I DO NOT *APPRECIATE* BEING TRIFLED WITH!!
IF THIS IS HOW YOU DO BUSINESS--
I QUI...!
CHK

READ THIS WAY
V...
XI!!
...
RINSLET...
I'M SO SORRY.
I'M AFRAID QUITTING ...
...IS NOT AN OPTION.

Chapter 70:
Cerberus

SLIP
V AND XI!!
TWO MORE AGENTS OF THE CHRONO NUMBERS ...!!

...
COMMANDER ...
IF THIS GIRL CAN'T KEEP HER *MOUTH SHUT* LONG ENOUGH TO HEAR YOU OUT ...
HMPH!
IS SHE WORTH THE TROUBLE?
...
WHAT DO YOU SAY, BELUGA?
...
HMPH! CAT GOT YOUR TONGUE AS USUAL, HUH?

NIZER!
DON'T UNDER-ESTIMATE RINSLET.
WHAT SHE LACKS IN REFINEMENT, SHE MAKES UP FOR...
...IN BOOBAGE!
WHACK!!
WHAT DID YOU JUST SAY?!
NIZER...
PANT
PANT
I APPRECIATE YOUR CONCERN.

BUT I'M THE ONE AT FAULT HERE.
I OUGHT TO HAVE BEEN MORE CAREFUL WITH MY WORDS.
PERK
...
MY APOLOGIES, MISS WALKER.
WHAT FURTHER BUSINESS?
THE FOOD SHOULD BE HERE MOMENTARILY.
LET'S DISCUSS OUR FURTHER BUSINESS, SHALL WE?
GURGLE

STOCK TOWN?
YES. IT'S A SMALL TOWN IN THE SOUTHERN REGION OF THE BELES REPUBLIC.
OVER THE PAST SEVERAL WEEKS...
APPROXIMATELY 20 SWEEPERS HAVE VANISHED THERE.
ALL OF THEM...
...WERE PURSUING CREED DISKENTH.
...!
THAT MEANS...

YES.
I BELIEVE IT'S LIKELY THAT CREED IS THERE.
I DO NOT INTEND TO LET THIS OPPORTUNITY PASS.
CERBERUS WILL BE DISPATCHED TO CONFIRM OUR THEORY.
CERBER-US?
THEN, IF IT'S FEASIBLE, THEY WILL PROCEED WITH CREED'S ELIMINATION.

JENOS, NIZER AND BELUGA...
TOGETHER, THEY ARE "CERBERUS," THE NUMBERS' OWN COMMANDO ARM.
A SPECIAL TEAM?
Him?
RINSLET...
I WANT *YOU* TO ACCOMPANY CERBERUS TO STOCK TOWN.

WE HAVE YET TO LOCATE CREED'S SAFE HOUSE THERE.
BUT I BELIEVE, WITH YOUR COOPERATION, WE WILL.
?!
HOLD UP! YOU CAN'T GIVE ME *ORDERS*, YOU KNOW!
WHY WOULD I...
YOU'VE ALREADY ENTERED INTO OUR EMPLOY ONCE, HAVE YOU NOT?
OF COURSE, THIS IS A *VERY DANGEROUS* MISSION.
IF YOU'RE TOO FRIGHTENED, I UNDERSTAND AND APPRECIATE YOUR HONESTY.
I'D MUCH RATHER YOU GIVE UP *NOW* THAN PUT CERBERUS IN JEOPARDY.
WH-WH...

READ THIS WAY
WHO DOES SHE THINK SHE IS?!
I SWEAR I'M GONNA...
GR GR GR GR GR
...
YOU HAVEN'T *TOUCHED* YOUR PLATE. AREN'T YOU HUNGRY?
SLAM
OKAY, *FINE!*
HUH?
LET'S SAY I GO AND WE NAIL CREED.
WILL YOU STILL GIVE ME *ANY* REWARD I NAME?
THOSE WERE THE TERMS OF MY CONTRACT, RIGHT?
...

OKAY, FINE! *THIS* IS WHAT I WANT--
DON
I WANT YOU TO *RESIGN* YOUR POSITION AS COMMANDER OF THE NUMBERS! *AND* I NEVER WANT TO SEE YOUR FACE *EVER AGAIN!!*
That's the deal!
Please don't put your feet on the table.
HUH ?
HM...
...

STOCK TOWN
I WARNED YOU, SWEEPER ...
YOU SHOULD HAVE RUN WHEN YOU HAD THE CHANCE.
OH!
OH!
SLIT

THK
BLOOP

AHH!!
BANG
AHHHHHHH!!!
BANG
BANG
SHK
!!!
WHOOSH

SLK
CRK
CRK
AHHH!!
AH!
AHH!!
I BELIEVE I'LL TAKE YOUR *BLOOD*, NOW THAT *YOU'RE* THROUGH WITH IT.

READ THIS WAY
SL LK
POOF
YOU OKAY, CHARDEN? YOU SEEM KIND OF GRUMPY LATELY.
I'M FINE...
USING MY POWERS LEAVES ME PARCHED, THAT'S ALL.
HA HA. YOU'RE A SCARY GUY, CHARDEN.
I'M BORED. SEEMS LIKE ALL WE EVER DO ANYMORE IS DEAL WITH SWEEPERS.
HOW DUMB ARE THE NUMBERS THAT THEY HAVEN'T FOUND US YET?
HUH?
THEY'RE NOT DUMB. QUITE THE CONTRARY.

IN NATURE ...
WHEN A HUNTER STALKS HIS MOST DANGEROUS PREY, HE'S CAREFUL.
HE WATCHES AND WAITS, CONSERV-ING HIS POWER.
ONLY WHEN HE'S *CERTAIN* THE MOMENT IS RIGHT, WILL HE STRIKE.
THE WAY YOU GOT IN THE COMMANDER'S FACE BACK THERE... I DIDN'T THINK YOU HAD THAT IN YOU.

READ THIS WAY

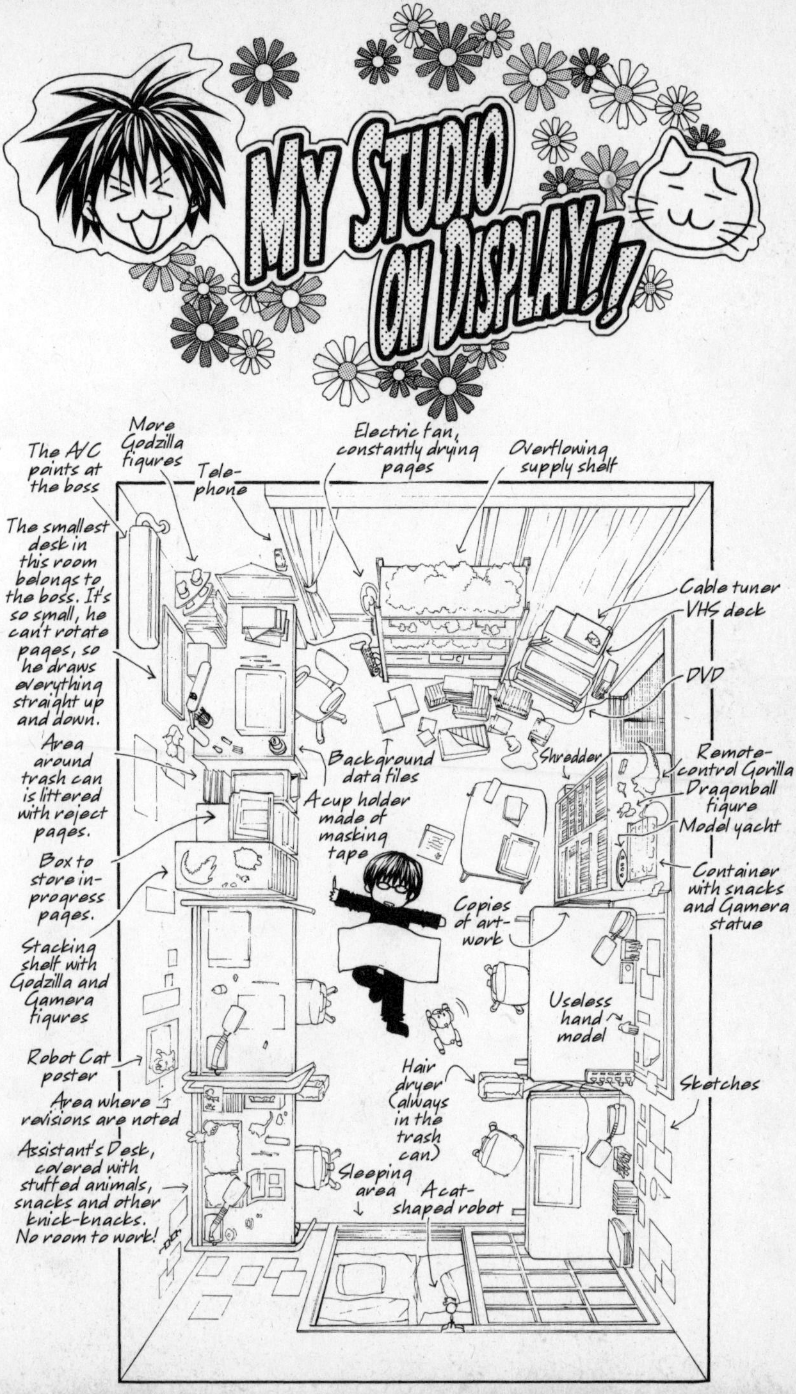
MY STUDIO ON DISPLAY!!
The A/C points at the boss
More Godzilla figures
Tele-phone
Electric fan, constantly drying pages
Overflowing supply shelf
The smallest desk in this room belongs to the boss. It's so small, he can't rotate pages, so he draws everything straight up and down.
Cable tuner
VHS deck
DVD
Area around trash can is littered with reject pages.
Background data files
A cup holder made of masking tape
Shredder
Remote-control Gorilla
Dragonball figure
Model yacht
Box to store in-progress pages.
Container with snacks and Gamera statue
Copies of art-work
Stacking shelf with Godzilla and Gamera figures
Useless hand model
Robot Cat poster
Hair dryer (always in the trash can)
Sketches
Area where revisions are noted
Assistant's Desk, covered with stuffed animals, snacks and other knick-knacks. No room to work!
Sleeping area
A cat-shaped robot

Chapter 71: The Mission Commences

DOCTOR ...
I NEED A FAVOR.
HOW CAN I HELP YOU?
I WANT YOU TO GO INTO TOWN AND BRING SOMEONE BACK HERE... AS MY GUEST.
A GUEST ?
DON

READ THIS WAY

Chapter 71: The Mission Commences

READ THIS WAY
OH, COME ON!
I AM SO SICK OF THIS!

WHY AM I THE ONLY ONE OUT LOOKING FOR LEADS?
THE MOMENT WE HIT TOWN, JENOS AND THE OTHER TWO VANISHED. POOF!
HEYA, BABY! ♪
WHAT'S THE MATTER? BOYFRIEND TREAT YOU BAD?
FLICK
YOU RECOG-NIZE THIS GUY?
REWARD
$30,000,000
HUH?
NEVER SEEN HIM BEFORE.
WHAT DO YOU SAY YOU AND I HAVE SOME FUN?
...

POW
DING DONG
NOT INTERESTED!
...
TEE HEE ♡
I SEE YOU, LITTLE SWEEPER!

LA TI DA ♪
WHAT THE ...?!
SPIN
♫
SAY HELLO TO KYOKO!
TA DA ♥

READ THIS WAY
!!
THAT GIRL ...
KYOKO ...
YOU'RE ONE OF THE APOSTLES OF THE STARS!
TEE HEE HEE
HUH ?!
I AM. AND YOU ARE SEVEN POINTS! ♡
LITTLE LADY SWEEPER, SAY GOOD-BYE.
TIME TO DIE! ♡

HOFF
SUPER RED-HOT FIRE-BALL!!
!!!
WUOOF

BOOOM
WUUFT
SHOOT!
I MISSED.
SLAM
HEY!
WHAT DID I EVER DO TO YOU?!

OH, IT'S NOTHING PERSONAL.
I'M JUST FOLLOWING CREED'S ORDERS!
WE'RE PLAYING A GAME! IT'S CALLED "SWEEPER HUNTER!"
I GET *ONE POINT* FOR EVERY SWEEPER I KILL! ♡
"SWEEPER HUNTER"?
YES.
ZAK
DOCTOR!
ALAS, MISS KIRISAKI...
THAT WOMAN IS NOT A SWEEPER.
!!

READ THIS WAY

MISS KIRI-SAKI...
YEAH?
I'M AFRAID I HAVE TO ASK YOU TO LET THIS WOMAN LIVE FOR THE TIME BEING.
CREED...
...WOULD LIKE TO SEE HER.

STEP STEP
I'M PLEASED YOU CHOSE TO COME QUIETLY, MISS WALKER.
YOU'RE THE FIRST OUTSIDER TO EVER SET FOOT IN HERE, YOU KNOW.
NOT THAT IT MATTERS.
I DOUBT YOU'LL *LEAVE* ALIVE.
THIS WAY, PLEASE.
...
AN OLD CASTLE NESTLED DEEP IN THE MOUNTAINS...
NOT AN EASY PLACE TO FIND.

Hmph!
BIP
BIP
SEEMS THAT GIRL KNOWS WHAT SHE'S DOING.
SO FAR, SO GOOD.

SEPHIRIA WAS RIGHT ON THE MONEY, AS USUAL.
CREED SEES SOME-ONE HE RECOG-NIZES...
HE GETS CURIOUS.
...
THE OLD KNIGHT IN SHINING ARMOR ROUTINE!
YOU DO THAT WITH ALL THE GIRLS.
Heh
LET'S GO.
TUG
I'M WORRIED ABOUT RINSLET.
SLIP

YEAH, BUT...
I THINK IT'S DIFFERENT THIS TIME.
HA!
YOU ALWAYS SAY THAT, TOO!
ALL RIGHT!
ZAH
YOU READY, BELUGA?
...

READ THIS WAY
FIRST, WE'LL NEED TO GET THROUGH THAT DOOR.
IT'S A BIT FAR.
THINK YOU CAN HANDLE IT?
SLIP
OH YEAH.
I CAN HANDLE IT!

BLACK CAT

profile

BELUGA J. HEARD

DATA	
BIRTHDATE:	DECEMBER 11
AGE:	29
BLOOD TYPE:	B
HEIGHT:	216 CM
WEIGHT:	109 KG
WEAPON:	VERETHRAGHNA (BAZOOKA)
HOBBIES:	ROCK-CLIMBING, SLEEPING
COMMENTS:	HEARD IS CERBERUS'S CANNON SPECIALIST. DUE TO THE SIZE OF HIS WEAPON, MOST OF HIS MISSIONS INVOLVE CONFRONTATIONS WITH ENEMY ORGANIZATIONS AND INTERNATIONAL DISPUTES.

CHAPTER 72:
CERBERUS STRIKES

MISS WALKER! IT HAS BEEN A WHILE.
DID YOU EVER IMAGINE WE'D MEET AGAIN?
I HOPED I'D NEVER SEE THAT UGLY MUG OF YOURS...
...EVER AGAIN.

...
SMIRK
STILL SPIRITED, I SEE.
...
LISTEN UP. AS SOON AS WE KNOW HE'S IN THERE, WE'LL LAUNCH OUR ATTACK...
WIPE HIM OUT.
WHEN WE'RE READY, WE'LL FIRE ONE SHOT.
THAT'LL BE YOUR CUE TO HIGHTAIL IT OUT OF THERE.
YOU CAN HANDLE THAT, CAN'T YOU?

YEAH, LIKE IT'LL BE THAT EASY.
AND NOW...
MISS WALKER...
TELL ME.
WHAT BRINGS YOU HERE?
TO WHOM DO I OWE THE PLEASURE?
...

BOOM

SHATTER

?!!!

RUMBLE
WHAT IS THIS?
OH! AN EARTH-QUAKE!
...
THAT'S MY CUE!
BOLT
RINSLET!

SHHP
SLIIIDE

ECHIDNA ...!

WHOOSH
CRACKLE
SWISH
ZAH
chk
chk

...
BZZZ
...!!
CREED.
THE BIG FISH HAVE TAKEN THE BAIT.

SHATTER
VERY GOOD.
HIC!
GAK!
?!

HUH ...?!
THERE'S NO WOUND ?!
BUT I WAS STABBED!
HEH
HUH?!
STEP
STEP
ZAH
HEH HEH

STROKE
IT SEEMS...
...I WAS *RIGHT* ABOUT YOU.
YOU'VE BEEN *MOST* HELPFUL, MISS WALKER. THANK YOU.
HA HA HA HA!

DASH DASH DASH
BIP
BIP
!
DOM

YOU MUST BE THE CHRONO NUMBERS.
THAT'S FAR ENOUGH.
AND YOU'RE AN APOSTLE OF THE STARS.
TRUTH IS, WE'RE ONLY AFTER *CREED*.
NO REASON TO FIGHT *YOU* IF WE DON'T HAVE TO.
ANY CHANCE YOU'LL JUST STEP ASIDE?

HA!
BUT YOU *WANT* TO FIGHT ME, DON'T YOU?
NUMBER V.
I CAN TELL BECAUSE I FEEL THE SAME.
YOU'LL HAVE TO GO THROUGH ME.
IN THAT CASE ...
LET'S DO IT.

YOU USE TONG FA?
DO YOU REALLY THINK YOU CAN DEFEAT *TAOISTS* WITH OUTDATED WEAPONRY LIKE THAT?
VOOSH
HUH ?!!

OUT-DATED, HUH?
WE'LL SEE ABOUT THAT!

AHHHHHHH!
BOOM
CLUNK
CLUNK

NICE!
LOOK AT THOSE THINGS GO!
SNAP
YOU UNDER-ESTIMATE THEM, MARO.
WAFT
THESE GENTLEMEN ARE NOT SWEEPERS.
THEY ARE THE CHRONO NUMBERS.

THRUST
I KNOW, I KNOW!

I DON'T LIKE GETTING KNOCKED AROUND LIKE THAT.
I'M ABOUT TO LOSE MY TEMPER.
...
HMPH!
CHK
THAT'S MORE LIKE IT.

BLACK CAT

profile

NIZER BRUCKHEIMER

DATA	
BIRTHDATE:	OCTOBER 5
AGE:	28
BLOOD TYPE:	O
HEIGHT:	184.5 CM
WEIGHT:	91 KG
WEAPON:	DIOSKOUROI (TONG FA)
HOBBIES:	DRIVING, SMOKING CIGARS
COMMENTS:	CERBERUS' LEADER. NIZER HANDLES CLOSE-RANGE ATTACKS; JENOS, MID-RANGE; AND BELUGA, LONG-RANGE ASSAULTS.

Chapter 73: The Apostles' Vicious Assault

FATTY?!
DID YOU JUST CALL ME A FATTY?!
YEP.
YOU GOT A PROBLEM WITH THAT?
YES, I DO!
I'M NOT FAT.
I'M BIG-BONED!
SURE YOU ARE...
YOU SEEM LIKE A REASON-ABLE GUY...
YOU! THE ONE WITH THE HAT.

READ THIS WAY
LET ME REPEAT OUR OFFER.
WE ARE ONLY INTERESTED IN *CREED.*
LET US PASS AND WE WON'T HARM YOU.
...
DON'T BE SILLY.
YOU ARE PART OF CHRONOS.
OUR MISSION IS TO *DESTROY CHRONOS!*

CHAPTER 73:
THE APOSTLES' VICIOUS ASSAULT

SO THESE MEN ARE PART OF CHRONOS?
THAT'S RIGHT. THE CERBERUS UNIT, A DIVISION OF THE NUMBERS. AH, MEMORIES...
OH, SO...
NUMBER VII, JENOS.
NUMBER XI, BELUGA.
AND FINALLY...

NIZER ...!
YOU'VE ALL COME TO KILL ME, HAVE YOU?
...
CRANK
OUCH!
DON'T TRY ANY-THING STUPID, GIRL!
NEXT TIME I'LL CUT YOU FOR REAL.

NOT THAT YOU'VE GOT LONG TO LIVE ANYWAY.
TUG
WHAT...
WHAT DID YOU DO TO ME JUST NOW?!
I OPENED A SORT OF... HOLE.
NOT IN YOUR BODY-- IN SPACE.
IN S-SPACE?!
ZIP
POKE

SLUK
?!
ZHTT
MY POWER ALLOWS ME TO MANIFEST A *GATE*-- A PASSAGE THAT CONNECTS ONE POINT IN SPACE TO ANOTHER.
AS LONG AS I HAVE THIS ABILITY...
NO ONE...
...CAN ESCAPE ME!

READ THIS WAY

WHOOSH
...
I DON'T LIKE BEING TREATED LIKE A CHILD.
WIND ?!
...!
HE MANIPU-LATES THE WIND.
THAT LITTLE KID...
THUNK
THAT LITTLE KID CAN START A TYPHOON!

READ THIS WAY
!!
WHOOSH

TINK
KA KA KA KA KA
AH!
CHK CHK

GRAVITY BOMB!!
SWOOSH
HMPH!
HEE HEE HEE.
LISTEN TO ME!
A *FATTY* IS A BIG, DUMB GUY...A LOSER.

READ THIS WAY
THUD
I AM NOT A FATTY !!
...
MM.
WHY SHOULD YOU TWO HAVE ALL THE FUN?

NOW IT'S MY TURN TO PLAY.
BLOOP
?!
WHAT IS THAT?
I CALL IT "BLOODY RAIN"!

WHOOSH
!
WHOOSH
WHOOSH
BOLT
CRACK
CRACK
CRACK
CRACK
CRACK

THUKK
PSH
DAMN!
PSH
TAP
HEH!
SO THIS IS THE POWER OF TAO. THIS IS THE FIRST TIME I'VE SEEN IT UP CLOSE.

READ THIS WAY
NO WONDER THE ELDERS ARE CONCERNED.
JENOS! YOU OKAY?
STEP
HEH. YEAH, NO WORRIES.
NO LITTLE BRAT...
...IS GONNA SHOW UP THIS OLD GUY!
GLARE

BLACK CAT

profile

LEON ELLIOT

DATA	
BIRTHDATE:	APRIL 15
AGE:	13
BLOOD TYPE:	O
HEIGHT:	145 CM
WEIGHT:	37 KG
HOBBIES:	READING COMICS (ESPECIALLY MANGA), COLLECTING ACTION FIGURES
POWER:	AIR
COMMENTS:	LEON IS CAPABLE OF BLENDING HIS *CHI* WITH THE ATMOSPHERE AND MANIPULATING AIR CURRENTS. HIS POWERS ARE EFFECTIVE UP TO A 25-METER RADIUS. HE ALSO LOVES TO RIDE HIS AIRBOARD AND IS ESPECIALLY GOOD AT RACING GAMES.

CHAPTER 74:
ENTER TRAIN
MILK

YOU...
...ARE GETTING ON MY NERVES!
SSS
I DON'T THINK WE CAN BE FRIENDS.
AH, THAT'S TOO BAD!
OH, WELL. WHO NEEDS AN UPPITY LITTLE KID FOR A FRIEND?
I DO LIKE UPPITY WOMEN, THOUGH. ♡
YES, I DO. ♡

READ THIS WAY
DO YOU KNOW WHY I JOINED THEM?
WHY I BECAME ONE OF THE APOSTLES OF THE STARS?
SPARK
WHY?
BECAUSE OF PEOPLE LIKE *YOU!*
BECAUSE I WANTED TO GET BACK AT ***STUPID GROWN-UPS*** LIKE YOU!
THAT SO?
SMIRK

OH, MY. ISN'T IT THRILLING, CREED?
SOON WE'LL HAVE OUR BATTLE AND OUR PROOF.
PROOF THAT THE APOSTLES OF THE STARS AND THE TAO ARE FAR SUPERIOR TO CHRONOS AND THEIR NUMBERS.
I WONDER ...
CERBERUS, AFTER ALL...
...HAS ONLY TARGETED ME.
?
...

WHERE'D THE DOCTOR GO?
I DIDN'T SEE HIM LEAVE.
SWOOSH
!

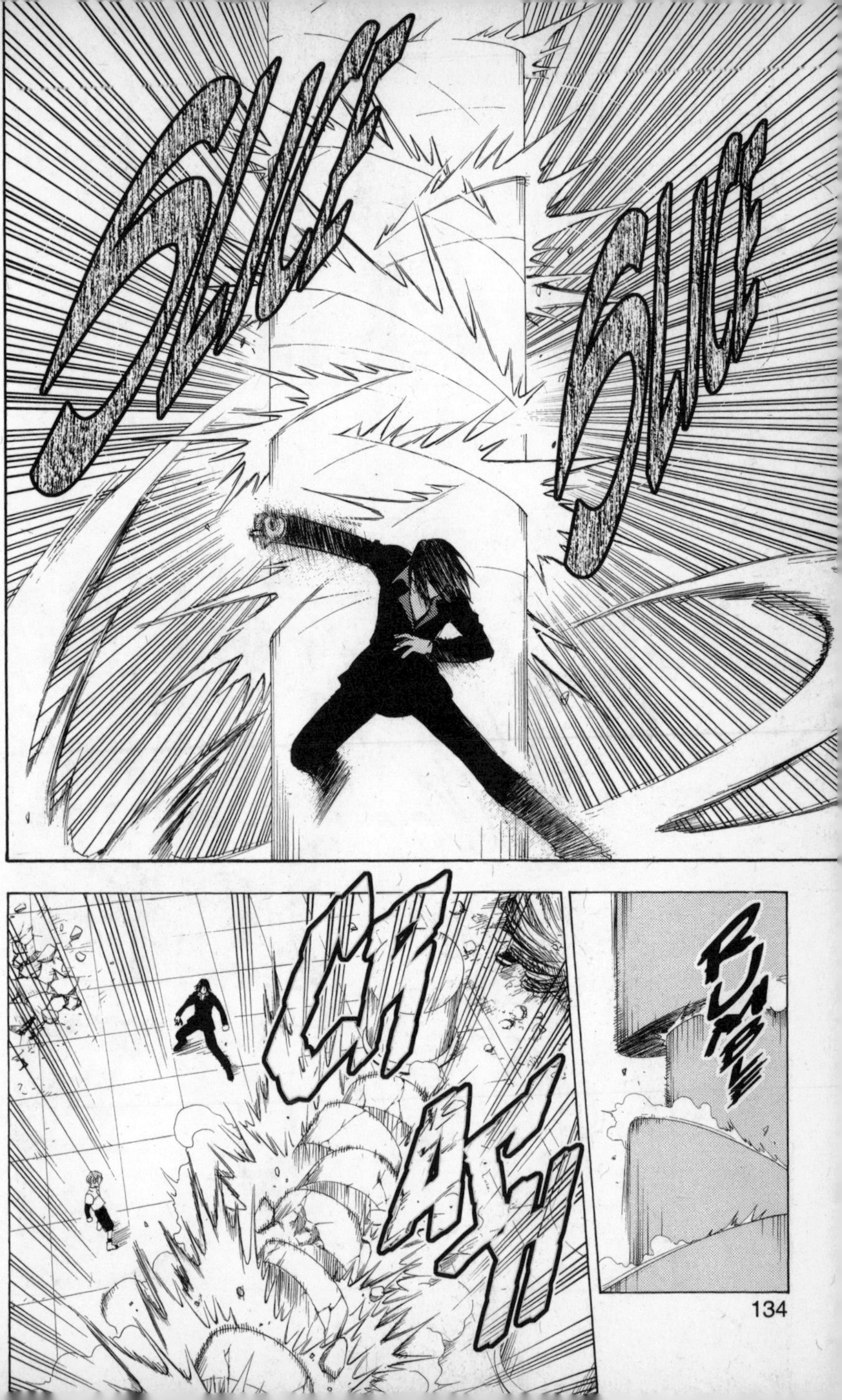
SLICE
SLICE
CRASH
RUMBLE

?!
CRASH
HOW THE ...?!
HE'S USING ...
WIRES!
NIZER! BELUGA !!
LET'S GO!!

SSS
SS
I'M NO LONGER ABLE TO SENSE THEIR PRESENCE.
HEH. I SEE HOW IT IS!
YOU GUYS THINK YOU CAN FOOL US WITH A SMOKE SCREEN, HUH?!
STEP
WHAT A JOKE...

VOOOSH
I JUST STIR UP A LITTLE WIND AND...
THIS IS NOTHING!
SHUU
...
?!

THEY'RE GONE.
WHERE'D THEY GO?!
...
THEY'RE HERE SOME-WHERE.
"WE'RE ONLY AFTER CREED."
DAMN IT!

READ THIS WAY
DASH DASH DASH DASH
HEH! ♡ SORRY, KIDDO.
THIS PART IS GROWN-UPS ONLY!

MEANWHILE IN STOCK TOWN, THREE KILOMETERS FROM CREED'S CASTLE--
HUH ?

SCORE
GAME OVER
WOW. YOU SUCK AT THIS, MISTER.
HAVE YOU EVER PLAYED A SHOOTING GAME BEFORE?
THIS IS SO WEIRD.
I MEAN, I'M PRETTY GOOD AT TARGET PRACTICE!
YOUR MISTAKE IS FIRING ONE-HANDED.
GIVE IT TO ME, I'LL SHOW YOU.
BANG
BANG BANG
KA-CHING

HMPH! KIDS TODAY.
WOW. THOSE LITTLE KIDS WIPED THE FLOOR WITH ME!
THOSE GAMES ARE REALLY HARD!
WE'RE SUPPOSED TO BE WORKING, NOT PLAYING. SVEN'S GOING TO BE MAD.
HOW CAN YOU WASTE MONEY WHEN WE'RE SO BROKE WE'RE LIVING ON INSTANT NOODLES?
OH, BOY! INSTANT NOODLES!
...

...
clack clack
clack
SVEN!
HOW'S IT GOING?
...
NOT GOOD. I SHOULD HAVE CHECKED THIS *TIP* MORE CAREFULLY.
?

WHAT?!
THE GUY WE'RE AFTER WAS ARRESTED TWO DAYS AGO?! AND HE WAS NOWHERE *NEAR* HERE?!
OUR INTEL WAS BOGUS.
WE CAME ALL THIS WAY FOR *NOTHING!*
PTOOIE
HA HA HA HA HA HA. THAT'S HILARI-OUS!!
HA HA HA HA HA HA HA HA
NO, IT ISN'T!

READ THIS WAY
WELL ...
CONSIDER-ING WHO GAVE US THE TIP, WE PROBABLY SHOULD'VE KNOWN.
YEAH, I SUPPOSE.
YOU GUYS!
YOU'LL NEVER GUESS WHAT I JUST HEARD!
...

WE RECEIVED WORD FROM ONE OF OUR AGENTS IN STOCK TOWN.
"TRAIN HEARTNET HAS BEEN SPOTTED."
THEY AWAIT FURTHER ORDERS.
VERY GOOD.
THE FALSE INFORMATION PLOY WORKED.

READ THIS WAY
EVERYTHING IS PROCEEDING JUST AS YOU PLANNED...
... SEPHIRIA.
...
I AM ORDERED TO *DESTROY* THE APOSTLES OF THE STARS.
TO COMPLETE THAT MISSION...
...I WILL BECOME THE DEVIL HIMSELF.

BLACK CAT

profile

ECHIDNA PARASS

DATA	
BIRTHDATE:	JULY 30
AGE:	?
BLOOD TYPE:	A
HEIGHT:	171 CM
WEIGHT:	46.2 KG
POWER:	GATE
LIKES:	WINE
COMMENTS:	CREATES "GATES" IN THE ATMOSPHERE, ENABLING HER TO PASS DIRECTLY FROM ONE POINT IN SPACE TO ANOTHER NOWHERE NEAR THE FIRST. (MORE DETAILS TO COME IN THE NEXT VOLUME!). BEFORE SHE JOINED THE APOSTLES OF THE STARS, SHE WAS A FAMOUS ACTRESS.

Chapter 75: Train Approaches

GLUG
GLUG
NO.
THAT WON'T BE NECESSARY, SHIKI.
WHAT?
BY NOW I'M SURE THE DOCTOR HAS BEGUN PREPARING...
...OUR EXPERIMENT.
...
CREED...
WHAT EXACTLY ARE YOU PLANNING?

Chapter 75: Train Approaches

SIP
YEAH, IT'S ME.
IT'S TIME TO BREAK OFF THE TRAIN HEARTNET SURVEIL-LANCE.
MOVE TO STAGE TWO OF OUR PLAN.
BIP

NOW...
WE JUST NEED TO LURE TRAIN TO CREED'S FORTRESS.
ARE YOU SURE ABOUT THIS?
SEPHIRIA?

SLURP
SLURP
SLURP
...
THEY'RE GONE.
KINGDOM NOODLE

YEP.
...
YOU MEAN THOSE PEOPLE WHO WERE FOLLOWING US?
!
EVE, YOU CAUGHT THAT?
I WASN'T SURE, SO I DIDN'T SAY ANYTHING.
NOT BAD, PRINCESS!
THOSE GUYS WERE PRETTY *GOOD*, TOO!

YEAH, THEY KNEW WHAT THEY WERE DOING, FOR SURE.
REALLY ?
WELL...
I CAN THINK OF A *NUMBER* OF POSSI- BILITIES.
...
WHO DO YOU THINK SENT THEM?
'SCUSE ME! YOU THERE!

CAN I TROUBLE YOU FOR SOME DIREC- TIONS?
I'M LOOKING FOR MIAN STREET, BUT I'M A LITTLE TURNED AROUND.
!
MIAN STREET ?
I THINK IT'S THAT WAY. I SAW THE SIGN EARLIER.
IS THAT SO? MUCH OBLIGED.
...
SLIP
HEY...

LET ME SHOW MY APPRECIATION...
...WITH A TIP ON THE WHEREABOUTS OF A *MASTER CRIMINAL!*
?!
HIS FACE ...?!
I KNOW *ALL* ABOUT IT.
YOU GOT A BAD LEAD, AM I RIGHT?

READ THIS WAY

ALL DONE.
TUG
GOOD WORK...

...NUMBER X!
NO WONDER THEY CALL YOU "THE MAGICIAN."
THAT'S ONE HELL OF A DISGUISE.

FUNNY THING IS, IT WASN'T REALLY NECES-SARY.
TRAIN HEARTNET DOESN'T KNOW MY FACE.
BUT...
SURE, WE WERE BOTH NUMBERS.
BUT I DIDN'T JOIN UP UNTIL HE'D ALREADY LEFT!

VROOM
SECTION K74291...
AM I REMEMBERING THAT RIGHT, SVEN?
YEP.
YOU SURE YOU WANNA DO THIS, TRAIN?
IT'S GOTTA BE A *TRAP.*
...

MAYBE SO.
BUT NOW I'M *CURIOUS.* I GOTTA FIND OUT WHO'S BEHIND THIS!
GRIT
TRAIN!
IT'S THAT ATTITUDE THAT ALWAYS GETS US IN TROUBLE!
HEE HEE! OH, C'MON! ADMIT IT, YOU'RE CURIOUS, TOO!
I AM NOT!

HUH?
WOW!
VROOM
SECTION K74291 ...
THIS IS IT!

IT'S A CASTLE!
MAN, THAT THING'S *HUGE.*
CLATCH
WE'RE GOING IN!
CAW
CAW
WHAT THE HELL HAP-PENED HERE?!
ZAH
...

8 Cerberus Strikes (The End)

「STRAY CAT」

◎ THIS IS A ONE SHOT THAT WAS PUBLISHED ABOUT SIX MONTHS BEFORE *BLACK CAT*. I WANTED TO SHARE IT WITH YOU BEFORE, BUT IT HAD TO BE POSTPONED DUE TO THE PAGE COUNT.

◎ "STRAY CAT" WAS A TRIAL VERSION OF *BLACK CAT*, SO THE SET-UP VARIES A LITTLE. TRAIN AND SVEN, FOR INSTANCE, ARE "DELIVERY MEN" INSTEAD OF "SWEEPERS." COMMON ELEMENTS INCLUDE THE CAT, GYANZA, THE SPECIAL GUN AND BOUNTY HUNTERS CALLED "SWEEPERS." I THINK IT'S KIND OF FUN TO COMPARE THE TWO.

◎ THERE ARE PANELS THAT I WAS TEMPTED TO RETOUCH, BUT FOR THE MOST PART I DECIDED AGAINST IT, SINCE I WAS DOING THE BEST I COULD BACK THEN. I ALSO THOUGHT YOU MIGHT GET A KICK OUT OF SEEING SVEN WITH THE BEARD, SO I LEFT IT.

BONUS STORY: STRAY CAT

TO TAOISTS LIKE OUR-SELVES...
YOU ARE NOTHING MORE THAN A PET!
A STRAY CAT...
...LIVES FREE!
$150000

BONUS STORY
ストレイ・キャット
STRAY CAT

POW
WHAT THE HELL?!
YOU SAID YOU HAD A *DELIVERY* FOR ME!
YEP! FROM A BROKEN-HEARTED WOMAN NAMED IRIS...
DON
DON
ONE KNUCKLE SANDWICH! SPECIAL DELIVERY!!
!
TRAIN HEARTNET
PROFESSIONAL DELIVERY MAN
IRIS...
?
...

READ THIS WAY
WHAT?
YOU OWE ME $15. THAT WAS C.O.D.
YOU THINK I'M GONNA PAY YOU?!
A DELIVERY MAN...
...TRANSPORTS AN ITEM FROM ONE PLACE TO ANOTHER, THEREBY EARNING HIS *FEE*.
SERIOUSLY, TRAIN...
FUU
IT DIDN'T *OCCUR TO YOU* THAT WE MIGHT NOT GET *PAID* FOR THAT JOB?
SVEN
TRAIN'S PARTNER
WHAT? WE DELIVERED. WE SHOULD GET PAID!
YANK
YANK
WHO WOULD *PAY YOU* FOR A PUNCH IN THE FACE?!

THAT'S HARSH, MAN.
YANK YANK
...
FROM NOW ON, MAYBE I SHOULD BE IN CHARGE OF WHICH JOBS WE TAKE.
GRUMBLE
I'M HUNGRY.
YEAH, WELL, WE'RE BROKE.
GET UP!
WHAT'RE YOU GONNA DO?
ZAH
HANGING OUT *HERE* ISN'T EARNING ANY DOUGH.
FREEK TOWN IS A HUGE CITY.
WE'RE BOUND TO TURN UP A DELIVERY OR TWO.
I'LL HANDLE IT. YOU JUST HANG OUT AND WAIT FOR ME.
OKAY!!
I'LL GO FIND SOME-THING TO EAT.

SOMETHIN' TO EAT...
BUZZ BUZZ
SOMETHIN' TO EAT...
MUTTER MUTTER
I AM DEBU
GONNA GET ME SOME MEAT.
I haven't had a piece of meat for two months!
MAYBE SOMEONE DROPPED SOME...
huff
huff
DASH DASH DASH
MAYBE I COULD CATCH A DOG...?
TOO BAD I'M ALLERGIC TO DOG!
!
HEY!
YOU WITH THE BED-HEAD!
HUH?
Me?

ZAH
PAY ATTENTION!
THERE'S A DAMSEL IN DISTRESS!
ZAH
ZAH
WHO'S THIS PUNK?!
UNLESS YOU HAVE A DEATH WISH, PUNK, GIVE US THE KID!

READ THIS WAY
KID?! WHY, YOU'RE JUST A BUNCH OF DUMB THUGS!!
THUGS ?!!
WAH WAH
IF I HADN'T FORGOTTEN TO LOAD MY GUN, I'D--!!
...
HEY! YOU'RE A MAN... DON'T YOU CARRY SOME KIND OF WEAPON?
I COULD USE SOME HELP HERE!
SURE THING! ♪
FOR A *PRICE,* OF COURSE.
A PRICE ?!
YEP!
LUNCH IS ON YOU!!
GRIN
There!
...
OKAY, I GUESS THAT'LL WORK.
YOU BETTER KNOW WHAT YOU'RE DOING!

OH, I DO.
SMIRK
HUH?!
C'MON!
LET'S DO IT!!
HEY!
VROOM
WHOOSH
WHERE'S HE GOING?!
WHAT ARE YOU DOING? RUNNING AWAY ?!!
YANK
YANK
OW! OW! OW!
I NEVER SAID I WAS GONNA FIGHT!
DASH DASH
DASH DASH

READ THIS WAY

YUP!
IT'S A TOUGH GIG.
YADDA
MY PARTNER LECTURES ME--
I'M ALWAYS HUNGRY!
WE'RE POOR!
DID I ALREADY SAY I'M HUNGRY?
YADDA
YADDA
AT LEAST I GOT TO EAT TODAY!
TALK ABOUT A WIND-DROP.
CHOMP CHOMP
THE WORD IS WIND-*FALL*.
ANY-WAY, SO WHAT?
YOU LIKE YOUR JOB, DON'T YOU?
YOU'RE SO... FREE!
PICK
I GUESS SO.
WELL, IT DOESN'T MATTER HOW FREE YOU ARE IF YOU LIVE LIFE HOLDING BACK!
GRIN
SWEEPERS KNOW HOW TO *LIVE!!*
!

READ THIS WAY
SWEEPERS?
YEAH!
YOU CATCH CROOKS, COLLECT REWARDS, AND BUILD A REPUTATION!
IT'S THE *ULTIMATE!*
SWEEPING...
THAT'S THE LIFE FOR ME!
RIGHT NOW, I'M STILL LEARNING THE GAME.
BUT ONE DAY, I'LL BE KNOWN THE WORLD OVER AS THE GREATEST SWEEPER EVER!
I'LL BE BIGGER THAN THE MOST LEGENDARY SWEEPER OF ALL!
THE *BLACK CAT!*
!

C'MON! YOU'VE AT LEAST HEARD OF HIM, RIGHT?
GOLDEN EYES? BLACK OVER-COAT?
NO TARGET CAN ESCAPE THE BLACK CAT. HE'S INFAMOUS!
ME?
A-HEM!
I'M GONNA BE *EVEN BIGGER!*
THUD
1 TON
AND YET A BUNCH OF SMALL-TIME THUGS NEARLY KILLED YOU.
pick pick
TH-THAT WASN'T ...
WHAT ABOUT YOUR FAMILY?
?!
WHAT DOES YOUR FAMILY HAVE TO SAY ABOUT THIS?
ABOUT YOU BECOMING A BIG-TIME SWEEPER?

MY FAMILY ...
...HAS NOTHING TO DO WITH THIS!
AS IF YOU COULD!
...
SLURP
YOU SEE...
HOT !!!
OW!
PBLLT!!
OW!
I forgot I can't take hot foods.
OW!
OW!
COUGH
COUGH
COUGH
...

CLINK
THANKS FOR YOUR HELP, DELIVERY MAN.
I'VE GOT THINGS TO DO...
I BETTER GET GOING.
SCOOT
OKAY, UH...
BIP
HELLO?
TRAIN! WHERE ARE YOU?
I GOT US A GIG.
REALLY?

YEAH, SOME RICH GUY IN THE SUBURBS ...
HE SAYS HIS DAUGHTER TOOK OFF THIS MORNING.
HE WANTS US TO DELIVER HIS LITTLE KITTY SAFELY BACK HOME.
A RUNAWAY? WHY NOT LET THE POLICE HANDLE IT?
BECAUSE!
HE'S OFFERING...
...$50 GRAND!!
$50 GRAND ?!
!!
YEP. HOW COULD I REFUSE?
ANYWAY, I'M SENDING A PICTURE OF THE GIRL TO YOUR PHONE.

BIP
!
HER NAME'S CHERYL KINNEAS. SHE TURNS 17 NEXT MONTH.
SHE AND HER DAD GOT IN A BIG FIGHT ABOUT HER FUTURE, SO SHE TOOK OFF.
SHE WASN'T CARRYING MUCH MONEY, SO SHE CAN'T HAVE GONE FAR.
SVEN...
YEAH?
THIS ISN'T GOING TO BE EASY.
BAR 猫魔人

READ THIS WAY

SWISH
...
LICK
SPLAT
SPLAT

OKAY. THIS TIME I LOAD MY GUN...
BEFORE I FIND MY NEXT TARGET!
...
ch-chk
NO FAIR!
YOU WERE A SWEEPER WHEN YOU WERE YOUNG, DADDY!
YOU SHOULD UNDER-STAND HOW I FEEL!

I MADE A PROMISE TO YOUR LATE MOTHER.
I PROMISED I WOULD RAISE YOU PROPERLY.
WHAT ABOUT MY DREAMS ?!
WHAT ABOUT WHAT I WANT?!
I WANT TO BE A SWEEPER AND...
THAT'S ENOUGH !!
!
HE PROBABLY THINKS I CAN'T HANDLE IT!
CH-CHK
MAYBE IF I PROVE I CAN DO IT...

SWAGGER
SWAGGER
SWAGGER
HM
...
GASP
GYANZA RUJIKKE ?!
HE'S KILLED 100 MEN!
THE BOUNTY ON HIM IS ENORMOUS!
AND THERE HE IS!

WHOOSH
HE'S MINE!!
FREEZE!!
...
LEAP
LEAP
ARF ARF ARF
ZINKAWA
?

READ THIS WAY

WHAT?
SEE SOMETHING YOU WANT, GIRLIE?
Th-thump Th-thump Th-thump
ULP
AS A MATTER OF FACT I DO!!
I WANT TO COLLECT THE *MILLION DOLLAR BOUNTY* ON YOUR HEAD!!

READ THIS WAY
WHAT?! YOU'RE A SWEEPER ?!
HERE'S A TIP, SWEEPER ...
IF YOU'RE GONNA POINT A GUN AT SOMEONE, BETTER MAKE SURE THE SAFETY'S OFF FIRST!
?!
GAH
OOPS!
UH OH!

WHOOSH!
!!!
AH...!
CHK
YOU'RE NEW AT THIS, HUH?
IF YOU WANT TO PLAY WITH THE BIG BOYS...
YOU BEST BE PREPARED TO *DIE!*
...

READ THIS WAY

!!!
DUUSH
MAN...
THAT'S THE LAMEST AFRO I'VE EVER SEEN.

READ THIS WAY

YOU INTERRUPTED MY FUN!
I DO NOT ENJOY HAVING MY FUN INTER-RUPTED!!
...
SCRITCH SCRITCH
WOW, THOSE ARE SOME SPOOKY EYES YOU'VE GOT THERE.
RUN, YOU IDIOT!
YOU'RE GONNA GET YOURSELF KILLED!
HEY...
QUIET, NOW!
!

READ THIS WAY

CHK
A *CHI* PISTOL ?!
WHERE'D YOU GET A WEAPON LIKE THAT?
SO.
YOU KNOW IT?
ANYBODY WITH A PRICE ON HIS HEAD KNOWS THAT GUN!
OF COURSE!
IT USES THE *TAO* PRINCIPLE OF *CHI* ENERGY.
THE SHOOTER AMASSES HIS *CHI* AND FIRES IT THROUGH THAT PISTOL!

ABOUT TWO YEARS AGO, THE SWEEPER WHO CARRIED THAT GUN UP AND DISAPPEARED.
HE WAS LEGENDARY. THEY CALLED HIM THE BLACK CAT!
!
BUT SO WHAT?!
YOU NEED YEARS OF TRAINING TO FIRE THAT THING!!
I BET A YOUNG KID LIKE YOU COULD BARELY GET OFF ONE SHOT!
WE'LL SEE ABOUT THAT.
IT IS TRUE...
THAT FIRING THIS THING WORKS UP AN APPETITE, THOUGH.

IS THAT SO?
GLINT
GO AHEAD, SHOOT. AND WHEN YOU MISS, I'LL BE READY FOR YOU.
SHEEEEN
BANG

READ THIS WAY
BOOM
DODGE
HA!! FOOL!
YOU'RE DEALING WITH GYANZA RUJIKKE! MANY A SWEEPER HAS FALLEN BEFORE ME!
I CAN DODGE A BULLET...
...LIKE I WAS BORN TO DO IT!

MODE CHANGE!!
BLADE!!

HUH?
CLASH
SWISH
HMPH ...
I JUST CAN'T SHAKE THE HABIT.

READ THIS WAY

DO NOT INTERFERE WITH THE DELIVERY MAN'S BUSINESS AGAIN.
YOU DON'T WANT ME TO LOSE MY TEMPER.
OR DO YOU WANT TO DIE?
!!!
HECH HECH

SLAM
...
ZAH
THOSE EYES!
SOB SOB
THE DELIVERY MAN--!
HE'S THE BLACK CAT!!

UM...
ARE YOU SURE IT'S OKAY TO JUST LEAVE HIM THERE LIKE THAT?
BUZZ BUZZ
YEAH, HE'S TOO SCARED TO MOVE.
THE POLICE CAN HANDLE IT FROM HERE.
WHAT ABOUT THE BOUNTY?
BUZZ BUZZ
I DON'T WANT IT.
I'M A DELIVERY MAN.
I DON'T TAKE BOUNTIES.
...
BUT, WHY...?
YOU'RE A LEGEND!
WHY QUIT?
...
THE BLACK CAT...
DIED.
TWO LONG YEARS AGO.
HUH?

ME?
I'M JUST A DELIVERY MAN.
CAREFREE AND EASY GOING...
LIKE A STRAY CAT!
AND SO...
HE *DELIVERED* ME BACK HOME, SAFE AND SOUND.
THE BLACK CAT.
NOT LONG AFTER THAT I HEARD A RUMOR HE WAS WORKING AS AN ASSASSIN FOR THE MOB.
PROBABLY JUST A RUMOR, THOUGH.

AFTER ALL THAT ...
I FINALLY UNDERSTAND DADDY'S OBJECTIONS.
I'M GOING TO LAY LOW FOR A WHILE.
I'M NOT GIVING UP ON MY DREAM, THOUGH.
AFTER ALL, ONCE I MAKE IT AS A SWEEPER...
I'LL BE OKAY.
PUTT PUTT PUTT
WHAT ?!
THAT GIRL *STILL* WANTS TO BE A SWEEPER ?!
DOESN'T KNOW WHEN TO GIVE UP, DOES SHE?

SHE SHOULD GET TO CHOOSE HER OWN WAY.
LIVE THE LIFE SHE WANTS TO LIVE.
YEESH!
WELL? WHERE TO NEXT?
TO THE OCEAN! I'M CRAVING FISH.
A PORT TOWN?
I'M BOUND...
...TO MEET THAT STRAY CAT AGAIN.
STRAY CAT (THE END)

IN THE NEXT VOLUME...

Team Cerberus has penetrated Creed's castle and made their way past the Apostles. Now they face Creed himself. But Creed still has many lethal tricks up his sleeve, as well as a hostage...Rinslet Walker. Will Train make it in time to save Rinslet from getting killed in the crossfire?

AVAILABLE JULY 2007!

Taking on the afterlife one soul at a time...
BLEACH
SHONEN JUMP GRAPHIC NOVEL
Tite Kubo
volume 1
ONLY $7.95
Manga series on sale now!
BLEACH © 2001 by Tite Kubo/SHUEISHA Inc.
viz media
www.viz.com
RATED T TEEN
SHONEN JUMP
MANGA

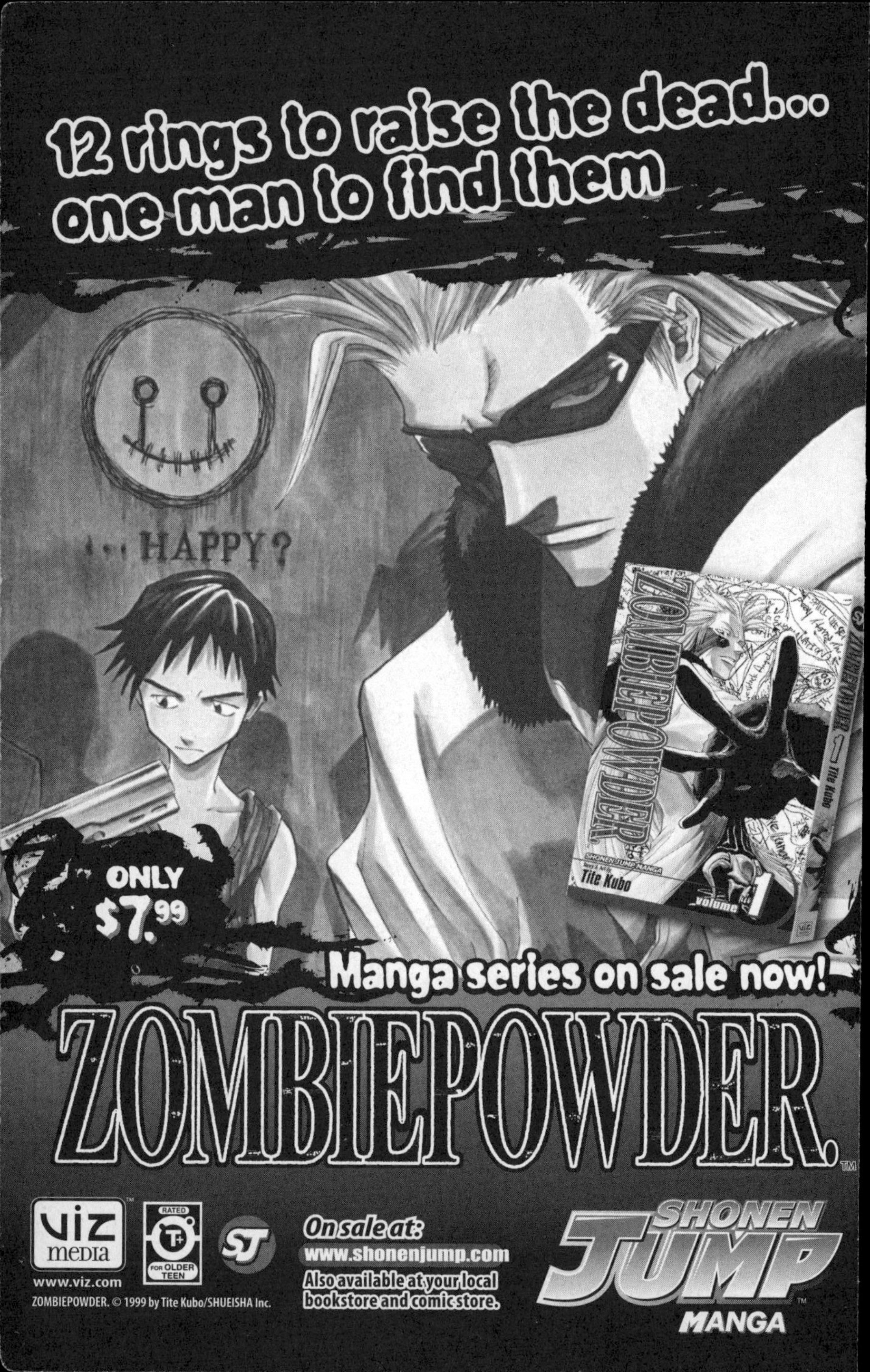
12 rings to raise the dead...
one man to find them
...HAPPY?
ONLY $7.99
Manga series on sale now!
ZOMBIEPOWDER.
viz media
www.viz.com
RATED T+ FOR OLDER TEEN
On sale at:
www.shonenjump.com
Also available at your local bookstore and comic store.
SHONEN JUMP MANGA
ZOMBIEPOWDER. © 1999 by Tite Kubo/SHUEISHA Inc.

Reborn will make all your death wishes come true!
ONLY $7.99
Manga series on sale now!
REBORN!
SHONEN JUMP ADVANCED
AKIRA AMANO
リボーン
REBORN!
TM
SHONEN JUMP ADVANCED
RATED T+ FOR OLDER TEEN
ATEKYO HITMAN REBORN! © 2003 by Akira Amano/SHUEISHA Inc.

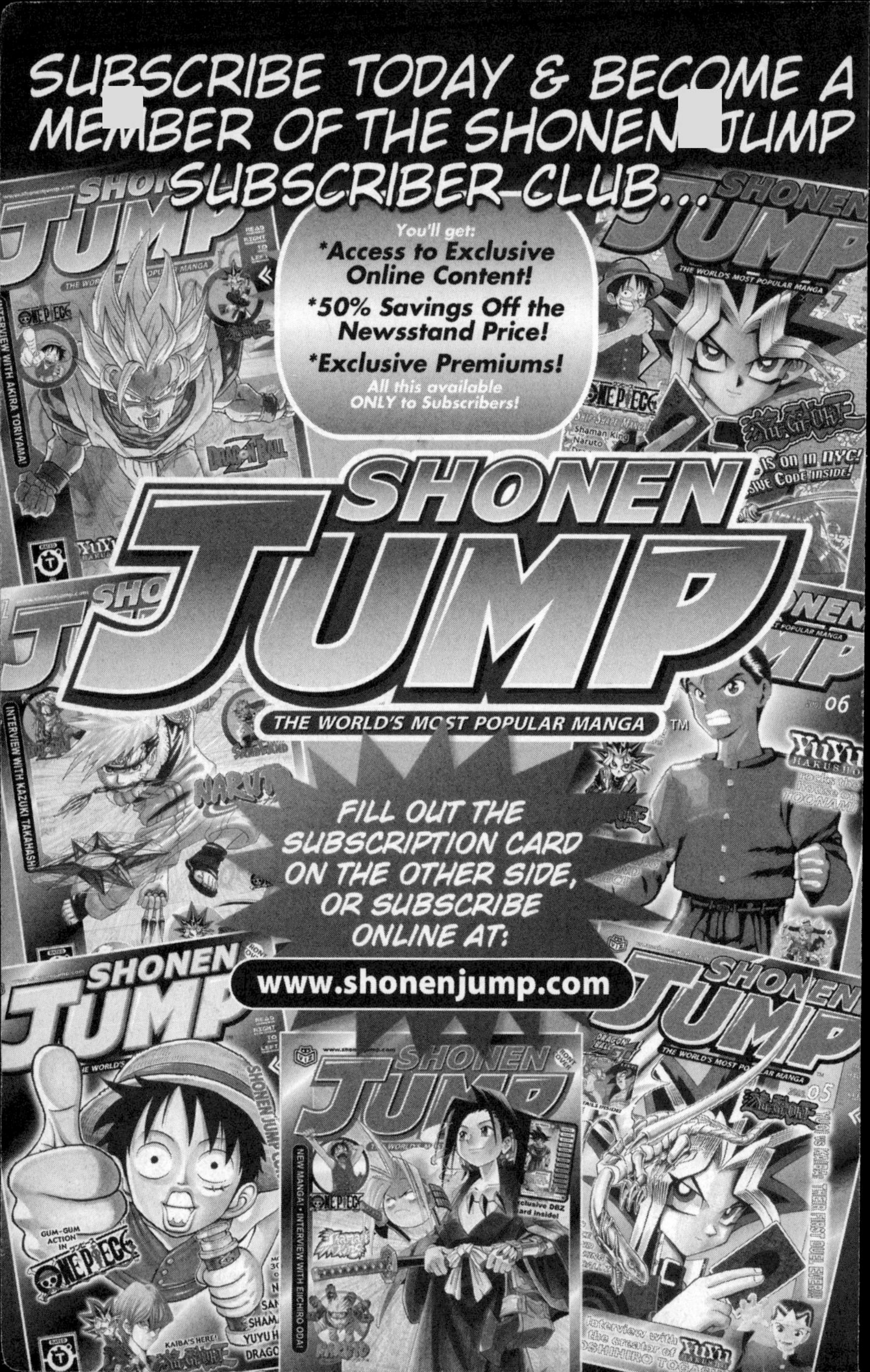

SUBSCRIBE TODAY & BECOME A MEMBER OF THE SHONEN JUMP SUBSCRIBER CLUB...
You'll get:
*Access to Exclusive Online Content!
*50% Savings Off the Newsstand Price!
*Exclusive Premiums!
All this available ONLY to Subscribers!
SHONEN JUMP
THE WORLD'S MOST POPULAR MANGA
TM
FILL OUT THE SUBSCRIPTION CARD ON THE OTHER SIDE, OR SUBSCRIBE ONLINE AT:
www.shonenjump.com